Electricity

Written by Sally Hewitt

W
FRANKLIN WATTS

First published in 2010 by Franklin Watts
338 Euston Road, London NW1 3BH

Franklin Watts Australia
Level 17/207 Kent Street, Sydney NSW 2000

Editor: Katie Dicker
Art Direction: Rahul Dhiman (Q2AMedia)
Designer: Shruti Aggarwal (Q2AMedia)
Picture researcher: Maria Janet (Q2AMedia)
Craft models made by: Divij Singh (Q2AMedia)
Photography: Divij Singh (Q2AMedia)

Picture credits:
t=top b=bottom

Cover: Tryfonov Ievgenii/Istockphoto
Title page: Tetra Images/Tetra Images/Corbis
Insides: Big Cheese/Photolibrary: 6, Nancy Catherine
Walker/Istockphoto: 7t, Deepbluephotographer/
Shutterstock: 7b, Richard Hutchings/Photolibrary: 8t,
2009Fotofriends/Shutterstock: 8b, Yuriy Tuchkov/
Istockphoto: 10t, Golovniov/Dreamstime: 10b,
Daniel Zuckerkandel/Shutterstock: 14, Michael
Svoboda/Istockphoto: 16, Helene Rogers/
Art Directors & Trip Photo Library: 18t,
Chen Ping Hung/Istockphoto: 18b, Daniel
Zuckerkandel/Shutterstock: 20, Ableimages/Riser/
Getty Images: 22t, Inga Nielsen/Shutterstock: 22b,
Tetra Images/Tetra Images/Corbis: 24, Ian Hamilton/
Istockphoto: 26t, Istockphoto: 26b, Paul Senyszyn/
Istockphoto: 27t.

Q2AMedia Image Bank: Cover, Imprint page,
Contents page, 9, 11, 12, 13, 15, 17, 19, 21, 25.
Q2AMedia Art Bank: 9, 13, 16, 17, 23, 27.

With thanks to our models Shruti Aggarwal and
Nazia Zaidi.

The equipment used for the activities in this book
can usually be found in your local hardware store.

A CIP catalogue record for this book
is available from the British Library.

ISBN: 978 0 7496 8760 1

Dewey Classification: 537'22

Printed in China

Franklin Watts is a division of Hachette Children's
Books, an Hachette UK company.
www.hachette.co.uk

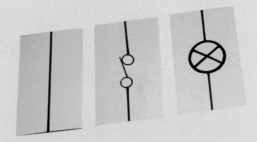

Contents

Words that appear in **bold** can be found in the glossary on pages 28–29.

What is electricity?

Electricity is a type of **energy**. Electricity is invisible, but we can see it at work all around us every day. It gives all kinds of machines we use the power to work.

Electrical energy

The electricity that comes into our homes is a type of electricity that flows. It flows along wires hidden in the walls and under the floors. We plug machines into **sockets** in the walls to use it.

Using machines

When machines are turned on, electricity flows from the socket, through the wire and into the machine. Machines change electrical energy into heat, light, sound or movement energy.

A hair dryer changes electrical energy into heat and movement energy.

How much energy?

Electric machines use different amounts of energy depending on what they are used for. Electric cookers, for example, use lots of electricity to heat food to a high temperature. Stereos use more electricity when the volume is turned up high than when it is turned down low.

An electric oven uses a lot of electricity to cook these biscuits.

Making electricity

The electricity we use in our homes is called mains electricity. It is made in **power stations** and travels through thick wires called cables. **Batteries** store small amounts of electricity. They are useful because they can be carried around. We use batteries to power laptop computers, radios, torches and many other things.

A mobile phone is powered by a battery so you can make a call wherever you are.

Safety!
Electricity is dangerous and should be treated with care. Never play with plugs or cables, which could give you a nasty **electric shock**, and even kill you.

Natural electricity

Static electricity is a type of electricity found in nature. Static electricity builds up because it does not flow. It eventually jumps from one material to another, such as from a wool jumper to a rubber balloon.

Making static electricity

Sometimes, when a jumper rubs against your shirt, it makes static electricity. You hear a crackle and you may see sparks. The static electricity makes the hairs on your arms and head stand on end! Rubbing a balloon against your jumper makes static electricity, too.

The static electricity on this balloon attracts the girl's hair.

Lightning is very powerful. You should stay indoors during a fierce thunderstorm.

Lightning

Lightning is caused by static electricity. When ice crystals inside storm clouds rub against each other, they create static electricity. If enough static builds up, a giant spark of lightning jumps between the cloud and the ground.

Make an electroscope

An electroscope detects (senses) an **electric charge**. If two objects become 'charged' with electricity, they move together or move apart.

Ask an adult to help you with this activity

You will need:
- card (10 cm x 10 cm)
- foil (14 cm x 14 cm)
- large paper clip
- sticky tape • glass tumbler
- blown-up balloon

1 Ask an adult to help you make a small hole in the middle of the card. Smooth out the foil. Cut two strips about 7 cm x 2.5 cm. Crumple the rest into a ball.

2 Open out the paper clip, leaving one end bent to use as a hook. Make a small bend about half way along the straight side. Push the straight end through the hole in the card and tape it in place on the bend.

3 Hang the two strips of foil on the hook. Place the card on top of the tumbler with the hook and foil hanging inside. Push the foil ball on top of the paper clip. Use the diagram below as a guide.

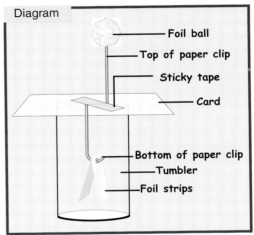

Diagram
- Foil ball
- Top of paper clip
- Sticky tape
- Card
- Bottom of paper clip
- Tumbler
- Foil strips

4 Charge a balloon by rubbing it against your hair or a sweater. Hold it near the foil ball. The static electric charge from the balloon causes the strips of foil to move apart.

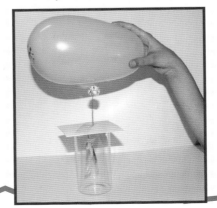

Batteries

Batteries are packs of electrical energy. Some batteries are thrown away when they have run out. Others can be **recharged** and used over and over again. Batteries come in many different shapes and sizes.

Chemicals and metals

There are **chemicals** inside batteries. When a battery-powered machine is turned on, the chemicals change and let out an **electric current**. When the chemicals have all changed, we say the battery has run out. It has to be replaced or recharged.

This camera is powered by four batteries.

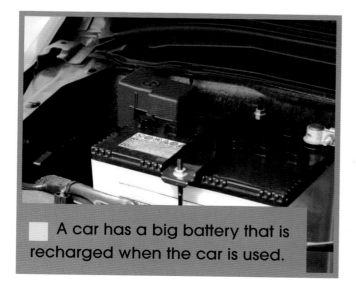
A car has a big battery that is recharged when the car is used.

Battery types

Torches use small batteries that have to be replaced. Mobile phone and laptop computer batteries can be recharged by plugging them into an electric socket. Car batteries are recharged when the engine is running.

Make a lemon battery

You can make a simple battery yourself using lemon juice (a type of chemical).

Ask an adult to help you with this activity

You will need:
- 2 lemons • 2 copper coins • 2 metal paper clips • insulated wire
- small light bulb in a holder
- insulating tape

1 Roll the lemons between your hands to release the juice. Ask an adult to cut two slots in either side of both lemons. Ask them to cut the wire into three lengths of about 25 cm and strip the ends to show about 1 cm of copper wire.

2 Push a coin and a paper clip into the slots in each lemon.

3 Tape the end of one wire to one side of the light bulb. Tape the other end to the coin in the first lemon.

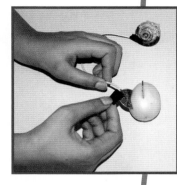

4 Tape the second wire to the paper clip in the first lemon and the coin in the second lemon.

5 Tape the third wire to the last paper clip. Now touch the end of the third wire to the light bulb. The light bulb should glow faintly.

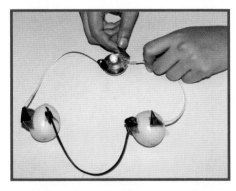

The lemon juice, the copper coins and the metal paper clips create an electric current strong enough to make the light bulb glow.

Current and circuits

Current is the way electricity flows. For a current to flow, it needs a **circuit** or a loop to flow through and a force from a power source, such as a battery, to push it along.

Sources of electricity

Power stations and batteries are two sources of electricity that make currents flow. Mains electricity pushes electric currents along cables and wires into machines that are plugged in. Batteries push an electric current through wires or metal strips to make a torch work, for example.

Metal strip

Battery

The battery in this torch joins up with a metal strip inside to complete a circuit.

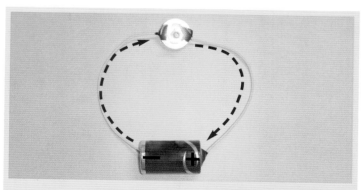

When a battery is connected into a circuit, the current flows round the circuit from the negative end to the positive end.

Positive and negative

A battery has a positive end marked with a plus (+) and a negative end marked with a minus (–). Batteries have to be connected the right way around in a circuit for the electricity to flow.

Make a simple circuit

Ask an adult to help you with this activity

You will need:
- 3 lengths of insulated wire
- 2 batteries (AA size)
- small light bulb in a holder
- insulating tape

1 Ask an adult to strip the ends of each wire to show about 1 cm of copper wire. Tape one end of two of the wires to either end of one battery.

2 Tape the loose ends of the two wires to either side of the light bulb holder. Does the light come on?

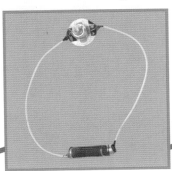

3 Add another battery to your circuit. Where will you put it? Will you need the extra wire? Which way around should the battery go? What happens to the light this time?

4 Draw diagrams of the circuits that made the light come on and the circuits that didn't. Add arrows to show the direction the electric current flows around the circuit from the negative side of the battery to the positive side.

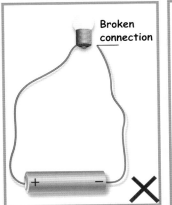
Broken connection

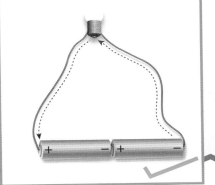

Circuits and switches

An electric current can only flow around a complete circuit. Electricity will keep flowing around a circuit until the circuit is broken or the energy runs out.

Power cut!

When there is a power cut, no electricity flows because the circuit has been broken. The lights go out and machines don't work. If a falling tree brings down overhead cables and breaks the circuit, for example, the electric current stops flowing.

On and off

We turn lights and machines on and off with a switch. When a switch is turned on, it connects a circuit so the electricity can flow. When a switch is turned off, the circuit is broken. A wall socket switch turns the mains electricity on or off by connecting or breaking the circuit.

During a power cut, the mains electricity doesn't work. We have to use torches or candles to read in the dark.

Make a circuit with a switch

Ask an adult to help you with this activity

You will need:
- small light bulb in a holder
- insulating tape • screwdriver
- wooden chopping board
- battery (D-type) • 2 drawing pins • metal paper clip
- 3 lengths of insulated wire (20 cm long) • stiff card
- pens or paints

1 Ask an adult to help you tape or screw the light bulb holder near to the top of the chopping board. Using the circuit below as a guide, tape the battery to the board.

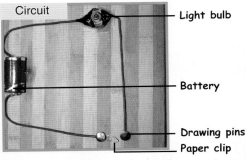

Circuit
— Light bulb
— Battery
— Drawing pins
— Paper clip

2 Push in the drawing pins the length of the paper clip apart, with one drawing pin going through the paper clip.

3 Ask an adult to strip the ends of the wires to show about 1 cm of copper wire. Tape the wires to the battery and the light bulb. Wind the wires around the drawing pins.

4 To turn on the light, touch the paper clip against the drawing pin. To turn off the light, move the paper clip away from the drawing pin to break the circuit again.

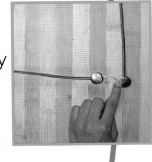

You can now use your circuit to light something up. You could make a lighthouse, for example, from a cylinder of card with a clear plastic cup at the top. Decorate your lighthouse with pens or paints.

Prop up the circuit board and stand your lighthouse in front of the bulb, so the light shines through the plastic cup.

Circuit symbols

A circuit can be simple with only three parts, such as a battery, some wires and a bulb. Or a circuit can have many different parts and **connections**. Symbols help us to understand the parts of a circuit and how to use them.

Recognising symbols

Symbols are simple pictures that you can recognise whatever language you speak. The symbols for a battery, a wire, a light bulb and a switch are clear and simple. They are recognised in many different countries.

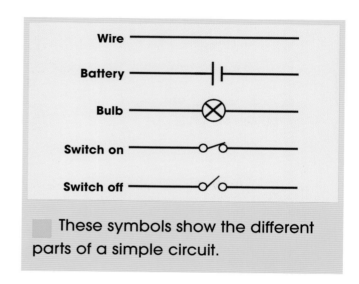

Wire	———————
Battery	——⊦⊦——
Bulb	——⊗——
Switch on	——o‾o——
Switch off	——o⁄o——

These symbols show the different parts of a simple circuit.

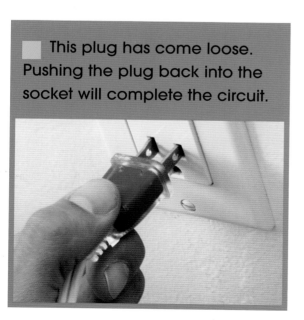

This plug has come loose. Pushing the plug back into the socket will complete the circuit.

Trouble-shooting

Every part of a circuit needs to be working for the electricity to flow. If a circuit isn't working, each part must be checked to find the cause of the trouble. Has the battery run out? Has the plug or any of the wires become loose? Is the light bulb broken?

'Complete the circuit' card game

You will need:
- 17 playing card-sized rectangles of plain card
- black pen • red pen

Play this with a friend. The winner is the first to complete a circuit! Your circuit will be made up of six cards – wire, bulb, wire, battery, wire, switch.

1 Using the box on page 16, draw the following symbols onto the cards: Wire x 8, Battery x 4, Light bulb x 2, Switch on x 2, Switch off x 1 (in red pen).

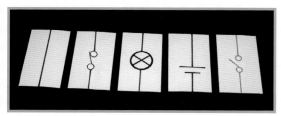

2 Spread the cards face down on the table. Pick up a card and put it down (face up) in front of you. Ask your friend to do the same.

3 Take turns to pick up a card. If your next card works with your first card, place them side by side. For example, a wire card will fit on either side of a battery, a light bulb or a switch card. An 'off' switch won't fit anywhere.

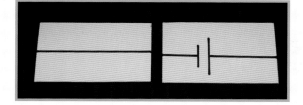

4 If the card doesn't go, you must put it back face down. Try to remember where the cards are on the table so you can avoid them or pick them up when needed.

5 The player who completes a circuit first shouts 'lights on!' Check that the circuit is complete. If it isn't, put all the cards back and start again!

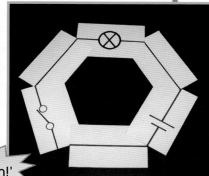

'Lights on!'

What are conductors?

Electricity can flow through some materials, but not others. Materials it can flow through are called **conductors**. Materials it cannot flow through are called **insulators**.

Conductors

Metals are good conductors of electricity. Wires and cables are made of metal so electricity can flow through them. Water is a conductor, too. Electrical machines should be kept away from water. If water gets on them they could give you a dangerous electric shock.

A cord switch in a bathroom stops you getting an electric shock if your hands are wet.

Plugs look different around the world, but have the same parts.

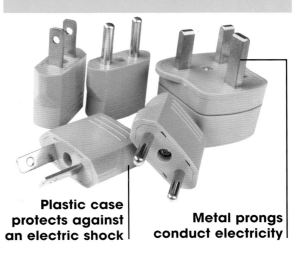

Plastic case protects against an electric shock

Metal prongs conduct electricity

Insulators

Rubber and plastic are insulators. Electricity cannot flow through them, so they are used to cover wires, plugs and switches to protect us from electric shocks. Metal wires and cables are coated in plastic. Electric plugs have a plastic or rubber case.

Test conductors and insulators

Ask an adult to help you with this activity

You will need:
- 3 short lengths of wire
- battery (D-type)
- 2 crocodile clips • insulating tape • small light bulb in a holder • objects made of different materials (such as a coin, metal teaspoon, paper clip, cork, pencil, strip of cloth, plastic fork)

1 Ask an adult to strip the ends of the wires to show about 1 cm of copper wire. Tape one end of two of the wires to either end of the battery. Tape the other end of one wire to the bulb and the other end of the second wire to a crocodile clip. Tape one end of the third wire to the bulb and the other end to the second crocodile clip.

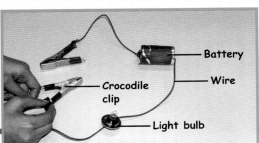
Crocodile clip — Battery — Wire — Light bulb

2 Use the clips to complete the circuit by attaching them to the objects made of different materials. Conductors will light the bulb. Insulators won't.

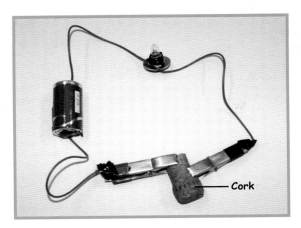
Cork

3 Can you guess which objects are conductors and which are insulators? Draw a chart to show your findings.

Object	My guess Insulator	My guess Conductor	Insulator	Conductor
Cork	✓	✕	✓	✕
Coin	✕	✓	✕	✓
Spoon	✓	✕	✕	✓

Making electricity

Electricity is made in power stations. Power stations burn **fossil fuels** such as coal, oil or gas, or they use **nuclear power**, to heat water. Steam from the water spins **turbines** that turn **generators** to create electricity.

Generators

Inside a generator, a coil of wire spins between **magnets**. This pushes an electric charge along and creates an electric current. A small generator can be used to make electricity in places where there is no mains electricity or when there is a power cut.

Sun, wind and water

Energy from the Sun, wind and running water can also be used to spin turbines, turn generators and make electricity. These **renewable** energy sources will not run out. They also work without burning fuels that **pollute** the air.

Wind spins the blades of these turbines and their generators turn to make electricity.

Make a wind turbine

Ask an adult to help you with this activity

You will need:
- square of coloured paper (20 cm x 20 cm) • ruler
- drinking straw • empty cotton reel • paper fastener • scissors • sharp pencil • lump of modelling clay • glue or sticky tape

1 Fold the paper in half diagonally from corner to corner and press along the crease. Repeat on the other side. Open the paper out.

2 Make a mark 4 cm from the centre point on each folded line. Cut along the folds as far as these marks.

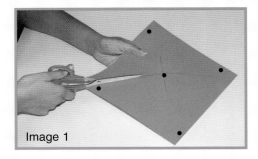
Image 1

3 Ask an adult to make a small hole through the centre using the sharp pencil, and a small hole in the corners (shown by the dots in image 1). Use the modelling clay as a support each time.

4 Bring the corners with the holes into the centre. Line up the holes, push through the paper fastener and secure it at the back. This is your wind turbine.

5 Glue or tape the back of the turbine to one end of the cotton reel. Push the straw into the hole at the other end of the cotton reel. Fix the modelling clay round the straw to hold the straw in place, leaving enough room for your turbine to spin.

Blow your wind turbine or hold it outside on a windy day. You could make and stick a cut-out paper butterfly to the cotton reel and watch it spin round.

Using electricity

Scientists have known about electricity for hundreds of years, but it wasn't until the 1800s that they found ways of making electricity and using it to power machines. Electricity changed the way people could do everyday things.

At home and school

Now we can plug in machines to play games and to send pictures and messages. At school, laptops can be used alongside exercise books, and interactive whiteboards instead of a whiteboard and pen.

Electronic whiteboards are now used in many schools.

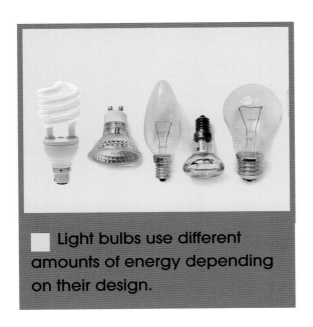
Light bulbs use different amounts of energy depending on their design.

How much energy?

The amount of electrical energy a machine uses is measured in watts (W). Old light bulbs use 60 W to heat up a metal wire, called a filament, to give out light. **Energy-saving light bulbs** use a gas instead of a filament. They only use 11 W so they are more energy-efficient.

Guess the power of electrical items

Ask an adult to help you with this activity

You will need:
- card • scissors • pencil and pens

1 Ask an adult to help you find the wattage of some everyday machines at home. You could also use the Internet to help you.

2 Make a chart to show your findings. Put the machines with the highest wattage at the top, and the machines with the lowest wattage at the bottom.

Machine	Wattage
Hair dryer	500 W
Television	340 W
Lamp	11 W

3 Cut the card into playing card-sized rectangles (two cards for each machine). Draw pictures of the machines onto the cards and label them. Write the wattage of each machine on the remaining cards.

4 Spread the cards out face-up on a table. Ask your friends to guess the wattage of each machine, match the cards and put them in order. Check their guesses against your chart.

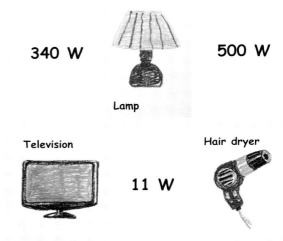

340 W   500 W

Lamp

Television   Hair dryer

11 W

Could you use some of these machines less often to save electricity? What would you use instead of the machines?

Saving electricity

Oil, natural gas and coal are formed from the remains of ancient plants and animals. One day these fossil fuels will run out. Saving electricity helps to save fossil fuels. It also prevents more pollution from burning fuels going into the air.

Motion sensors

Everyone can help to make an energy-saving plan and then find ways of making sure it works. Businesses sometimes install motion sensors to save electricity. The sensors turn lights on when someone is moving about, but turn them off when the movement stops.

Don't waste it

Electricity can also be saved by turning off lights and by fitting energy-saving light bulbs. Turning televisions and computers off completely helps to save electricity. Cooking several dishes at once makes the best use of an electric oven.

Pressing the off button on the television turns it off so it doesn't waste electricity on stand-by.

Make an electricity-saving switch

Ask an adult to help you with this activity

You will need:
- stiff A4 card
- strips of aluminium foil
- glue
- insulating tape
- 3 lengths of insulated wire
- 9-V battery
- small light bulb in a holder

1 Fold the card in half widthways, and open it out again.

2 Wrap a strip of foil all the way around each end of the card and glue the strips in place.

3 Make a circuit with the wires, battery and light bulb. Use the photograph below as a guide. Tape the two ends of the wires to the two pieces of foil.

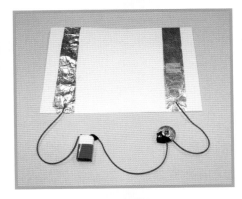

4 Press the card together so the strips of foil meet. This will complete the circuit and turn the light on. Let go and the light will go out. The light will turn off when you don't need it!

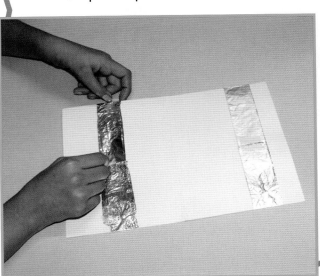

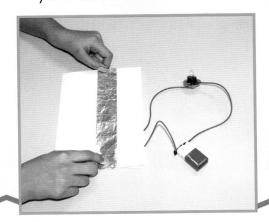

Keeping safe

Electricity is very powerful. An electric shock can kill or injure you badly. Always remember the rules and you will be able to use electricity safely.

Pylons and cables

Pylons carry electric cables above the ground. Signs give warnings that the electricity in the cables is very dangerous. It can kill anyone who touches a cable. Never climb or go near a pylon. Don't fly a kite near overhead cables.

DANGER OF DEATH

This sign is a warning about the dangers of electricity. It tells you to stay away!

Damaged cables are dangerous. They should be replaced before using electrical equipment.

Safety at home

If you see a wire showing through a cable or a plug, don't turn the machine on. You could get an electric shock. Tell an adult straight away. Never play with a wall socket or push anything into one. Always make sure your hands are dry when you use anything electric.

Design a safety leaflet

Design a leaflet about using electricity safely at home, at school and out and about.

Look back through this book for the safety information to help you. What could you tell your friends about the dangers of electricity?

Electricity safety tips

Keep safe at home

Dry your hands before touching a switch!

Keep safe at school

Keep electric cables tidy!

Keep safe out and about

Don't fly kites near overhead cables.

Glossary

battery

A battery is a small pack of electrical energy used to power some machines.

chemicals

Chemicals are substances that can combine to produce a chemical reaction.

circuit

A circuit is a complete loop around which electricity flows.

conductor

A conductor is a material that an electric current can flow through.

connections

Electrical connections are made when conductors, such as wires, are joined together and create a path for electricity to flow along.

electric charge

A material that holds or stores electricity is said to have an electric charge.

electric current

An electric current is a flow of electricity through a conductor, such as a wire.

electric shock

An electric shock is a sudden, painful and dangerous shock caused by an electric current flowing through your body.

energy

Energy is what gives people, animals and machines the power to work. Electricity is a type of energy.

energy-saving light bulb

An energy-saving light bulb is one that uses a gas, instead of a hot metal filament, to give out light. This helps to save electricity.

fossil fuels

Fossil fuels, such as oil, natural gas and coal, were formed from the remains of ancient plants and animals.

generator

A generator is a machine that uses a magnet to turn movement energy into electricity.

insulator

An insulator is a material that an electric current cannot flow through easily.

magnet

Magnets attract or pull magnetic materials, such as iron, towards them.

nuclear power

Nuclear power is a type of energy made in a nuclear power station, which is used to generate electricity.

pollute

To pollute is to make the natural environment dirty or to harm it.

power station

A power station is a place where electricity is made.

pylon

A pylon is a metal tower that holds up electricity cables running from power stations to people's homes.

recharge

To recharge is to put back electrical power into a battery.

renewable

Something that is renewable can be replaced or will not run out. Wind power is renewable.

socket

An electrical socket is a hole that a plug is pushed into so electricity can flow through the plug.

static electricity

Static electricity is still electricity. It doesn't flow. Lightning is caused by a build-up of static electricity.

turbine

A turbine has blades that are spun round by steam, wind or water to create movement energy that helps to generate electricity.

Index